Science Concepts
SECOND SERIES

Symbiosis

Alvin Silverstein, Virginia Silverstein, and Laura Silverstein Nunn

Twenty-First Century Books
Minneapolis

Twenty-First Century Books
A division of Lerner Publishing Group, Inc.
241 First Avenue North
Minneapolis, Minnesota 55401 U.S.A.

Website address: www.lernerbooks.com

Library of Congress Cataloging-in-Publication Data

Silverstein, Alvin
    Symbiosis / Alan Silverstein, Virginia Silverstein and Laura Silverstein Nunn.
        p.   cm. — (Science Concepts)
    Includes bibliographical references and index.
    Summary: Discusses the three kinds of symbiosis: mutualism, commensalism,
and parasitism and describes examples of these relationships.
    ISBN: 978–0–8225–6799–8 (lib. bdg. : alk. paper)
    1. Symbiosis—Juvenile literature. [1. Symbiosis.] I. Silverstein. Virginia B.
II. Nunn, Laura Silverstein. III. Title. IV. Series: Silverstein, Alvin. Science
concepts.
    QH548.S545 2008
    577.8'5—dc22   2007003184

Manufactured in the United States of America
1 2 3 4 5 6 – DP – 13 12 11 10 09 08

Contents

Imagine a world where hungry sharks and tiny fish can live a peaceful existence together. How about man-eating crocodiles and tiny birds? These animal relationships may be hard to believe, but they actually occur. Some plants even have ants as bodyguards to attack intruders. In nature many strange relationships occur in which different kinds of animals, plants, and other organisms in the five kingdoms of life come together for the benefit of at least one partner.

Animal partnerships are very important to many species because their survival depends on the association. But other partnerships occur because of a chance meeting that may be helpful for one or both of the partners.

A Taste of Honey

The honeyguide, a tiny African bird, forms a strange partnership with the ratel, or honey badger, a short, stocky animal. The honeyguide belongs to the

A honeyguide (left) *will lead a ratel* (right) *to a bees' nest to break it open so both can enjoy the honey inside.*

woodpecker family. Its diet consists of larvae (the wormlike young of bees, wasps, and termites), and it also feasts on bits of waxy honeycomb. But this small, delicate bird is not strong enough to break open the bees' nest to get at the honeycomb inside. The ratel, which belongs to the weasel family, loves to eat honey—and bees too. The ratel is well equipped to steal honey from beehives. Its long, sharp claws could easily tear a bees' nest open. Its heavy fur and thick, tough skin protect it from the stings of angry bees.

The honeyguide and ratel work together as a team to find a bees' nest and feast on it. When the honeyguide spots a bees' nest, it searches for a ratel. The bird flutters around the ratel's head, chirping away to get its attention. The ratel follows its guide to the nest, then breaks it open and feasts on the honey and bee grubs. When the ratel is satisfied, it is the honeyguide's turn to eat.

If the honeyguide cannot find a ratel to attack the nest, any other willing animal will do. Even humans have learned to follow this keen-eyed bird. A person will break open a bees' nest, collect some fresh honey, and leave enough behind for the little helper.

The honeyguide also forms associations with other kinds of creatures. Although the bird loves to eat beeswax, it cannot digest it. But millions of bacteria, creatures so small that they can be seen only with a microscope, live in its intestines. They break down the wax into simple chemicals that the bird can digest. Both partners benefit from the association. The bacteria get food and shelter, and the honeyguide gets nourishment from the wax.

The honeyguide is also involved in a one-sided partnership. Unlike most birds, the female honeyguide does not build a nest, sit on her eggs, and feed her young. Instead, she finds a nest made by another bird and lays a single egg in it when the other mother is not around. When the honeyguide egg hatches, the baby bird is blind and hungry and almost helpless. But it has two sharp hooks on its bill. It uses them to bite the other nestlings to death. The foster mother bird works hard and gathers food for a baby that does not even belong to her, while her own young have been killed. This is a one-sided partnership indeed!

One Smart Bird

The honeyguide is not the only bird that seeks parenting partnerships. Some other kinds of birds trick birds of other species into raising their young. One trickster is the common American cowbird that lives in the eastern United States. But some kinds of birds, such as the yellow warbler, have learned to outsmart the cowbird.

When a cowbird places its egg in the nest of a yellow warbler, the warbler can tell that an unfamiliar egg is there. The warbler then builds a new nest above the first one and leaves all the eggs in the first nest untouched, both hers and the strange one. If the cowbird comes back and leaves another egg behind in the second nest, the warbler will build a third nest above the second one. Usually the warbler manages to outlast the cowbird and finishes with a nest containing only her own eggs.

Living Together

In some cases, such as the honeyguide and the bacteria, different kinds of creatures actually live together for long periods of time, with one or both benefiting from the association. In other cases, partners will come together from time to time to help one another, such as the honeyguide and

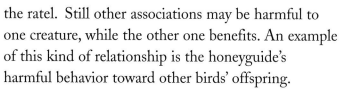

the ratel. Still other associations may be harmful to one creature, while the other one benefits. An example of this kind of relationship is the honeyguide's harmful behavior toward other birds' offspring.

However, there is usually some form of benefit for at least one partner in all of nature's partnerships. Animals and plants team up with other species that can provide them with food, shelter, protection, or transportation. They may even contribute to the reproduction of their partners (as when insects and other animals help to pollinate plants). Partnerships between species may include one or more of these benefits.

Scientists call nature's unusual partnerships symbiosis, which comes from two Greek words: *sym* (together) and *bios* (life). The term *symbiosis* refers to the living arrangements among organisms in all five kingdoms of life—animals, plants, fungi, monerans, and protists. An organism that lives with or cooperates with another species is called a symbiont. Some symbionts are so interdependent that they would die without one another. Others can survive without their partners, but they may become unhealthy or uncomfortable. Three kinds of symbiosis exist—mutualism, commensalism, and parasitism.

Mutualism is a partnership that benefits both organisms. An example of mutualism is the case of the honeyguide and ratel, where the animals have a mutual gain.

Commensalism refers to a partnership where only one member benefits, while the other is neither

This bull shark plays host for the remora attached to the side of its head. The remora uses the shark as transportation and protection.

harmed nor helped. *Commensal* means "dining at the same table," with one animal serving as a host and providing its guest with food, transportation, protection, or shelter. A shark, for example, is the host for the remora fish, which hitches a ride on the shark's body and snatches scraps of food along the way.

Parasitism is an association where only one organism benefits, while the other is harmed. The creature that benefits is called a parasite, and the other, at whose expense it lives, is known as its host. The honeyguide acts as a parasite on other birds when she lays her eggs in their nests. Certain bacteria (single-celled organisms) in our bodies that make us ill are also parasites. Not all bacteria are parasites, however. Some bacteria are actually helpful to other organisms. For example, some kinds of bacteria live in our stomachs and break down food, allowing our bodies to digest it more easily.

The term *symbiosis* was first used in the late nineteenth century by a German scientist, Heinrich Anton de Bary. He contributed to the discovery that in lichen, two different kinds of organisms can live and work together for the benefit of both. Lichen are hardy forms of plant life that grow in barren lands, in fields, in the woods, on rocks, and on tree trunks.

For centuries scientists believed that a lichen was a single kind of plant. When they studied these growths under a microscope, however, they discovered that lichen are really composed of two very different species. One, an alga, is a tiny green

Lichen can be found in many shapes and sizes and can grow in many places, including cold, treeless plains called tundras.

plantlike organism that can make its own food. The other, a fungus, is not green and cannot make its own food. The two species work together, and both benefit from the association. The alga provides enough food for both. The fungus provides shelter so that the alga can get the sunlight it needs to live and grow.

As scientists explore the world of nature, they are discovering more and more ways in which different species depend on one another and live together for the benefit of at least one of them. Nature's partnerships are sometimes very unusual, but they can be very important to ensure survival for many species.

The green ball in the center of this highly magnified photograph is an alga cell. The brown rods are the fungi that live with it in the lichen.

Symbiotic relationships can be found among many species all over the world. It does not matter how big or small the creature is. A huge hippo, for example, may have small birds called oxpeckers perched on its back, picking parasites off its skin. Other symbionts, such as the flea, are even smaller. The tiny flea latches onto a host, typically much larger than itself, and feeds on its blood.

We can see many associations in nature between different types of animals. But some living organisms are so tiny that we can see them only with a microscope. These creatures are called microorganisms. Microorganisms can live anywhere, even inside our bodies. Millions and millions of bacteria live inside our intestines. Bacteria are often considered bad or harmful. It is true that some bacteria are germs that can make people very sick. But most bacteria do not harm us at all. In fact, some of them help us.

The survival of many species depends on the presence of bacteria. Certain bacteria that live in our intestines, known as intestinal microflora, help to

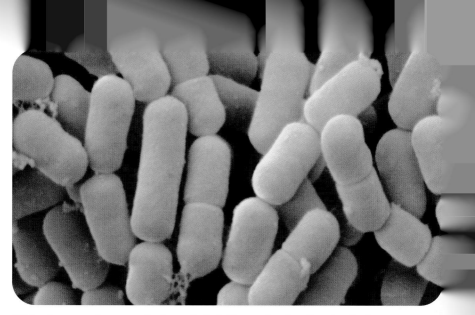

This close-up photograph shows helpful bacteria that live in the human digestive track.

destroy other organisms that could be harmful. Some microflora break down food to make it easier to digest. Yet others make important vitamins, such as different kinds of B vitamins and vitamin K, that make us healthy and strong. When we take antibiotics, we may get an upset stomach and diarrhea. This is because the medicine kills *all* the bacteria in our intestines—both the disease-causing ones and the helpful ones—eliminating important sources of vitamins from our body. The doctor may prescribe a vitamin supplement to replace the vitamins we lost because of the medicine.

Making Food Useful

All plant eaters, or herbivores, also need the help of microscopic partners to aid with digestion. A cow would starve to death in a meadow full of grass if it did not have helpful bacteria living in its stomach. Unlike the bacteria in our intestines, a cow's tiny symbionts make special chemicals. They help to break down grass into simple foods that the cow can digest.

Grass is made up of cells that contain many nourishing things, such as fats, proteins, vitamins, and minerals. But these food substances are locked inside the cells by a tough wall made of a material called cellulose. The cow cannot break down the cellulose to get to the important nutrients without the bacteria's help.

A cow has a four-part stomach. The first part, or chamber, is a pouch called the rumen. This is a home for millions of bacteria. When the cow swallows, the

A Cow's Stomach

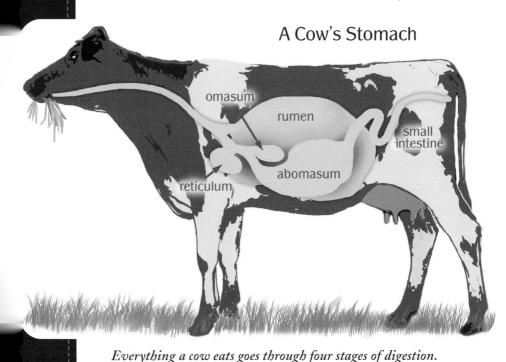

Everything a cow eats goes through four stages of digestion.

partly chewed mouthful of grass goes into the rumen. The cow's microscopic partners produce chemicals that break down the tough cellulose in the grass.

After the food has been in the rumen for a few hours, the cow burps up a mouthful of the partly digested material (called the cud) and chews it again. When the cud is swallowed, it passes into the second stomach chamber, the reticulum, for more digestion. Then it is sent to the omasum and abomasum to complete the process. Meanwhile, the cow is bringing up more cud, chewing it, and swallowing it.

The bacteria in a cow's stomach live only about twenty hours. But by the time they die, they have produced more bacteria to take their place. The dead bacteria pass through the cow's stomach and intestines and get digested along with the food. In this way, the dead bacteria provide extra proteins and vitamins for their host in return for the food and shelter they received when they were alive.

Rabbits also need the help of microscopic partners to digest the cellulose in the plants they eat. Instead of a multipart stomach, rabbits have a special pouch in their intestine, called the caecum. Bacteria that live in the caecum are able to break down the cellulose.

Rabbits eliminate the undigested remains of their food in the form of pellets, which are also filled with bacteria. The rabbits would lose the valuable vitamins and other nutrients in their wastes if it were not for a curious habit. They eat the pellets, giving the food another chance for digestion. Pet rabbits raised in cages with a wire floor, preventing them from picking up their droppings, may suffer from vitamin deficiencies.

Partners through the Ages

Scientists believe that some important parts of the cells of animals and plants were once bacteria. They were captured by some long-ago ancestor of present-day species and then were passed on by their hosts from generation to generation.

One important type is the mitochondria, found in the cells of virtually all eukaryotes. These are organisms whose cells have a nucleus. They include plants, animals, fungi, and protists. Mitochondria are football-shaped structures that burn food materials to release energy for the cell's activities. Researchers have found that mitochondria have their own DNA (the chemical that contains instructions for inherited traits). It is different from the cell's DNA, which is specific for the type of plant or animal. In fact, it is somewhat like the DNA of bacteria.

Chloroplasts are another kind of structure and are found in plant cells. They can use the energy of sunlight to make food by combining carbon dioxide and water into sugars. These, too, are believed to have started out as bacteria.

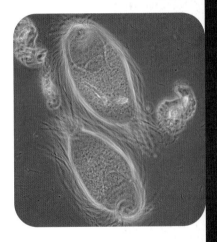

Termites (above) *have a symbiotic relationship with one-celled protozoa* (right), *which live inside termites and help them digest cellulose.*

Wood is another source of cellulose. Insects called termites feed on wood. Swarms of termites make their nests inside trees or in the wood frames of people's houses. Although termites can do terrible damage to people's homes, they do an important job in the forest. They break down old dead logs and branches, making room for new plant life to grow.

Like cows and rabbits, termites cannot digest cellulose all by themselves. Termites have microscopic symbionts living inside them, but they are not bacteria. They are tiny one-celled protozoa, which are animal-like creatures. Scientists call them flagellates because they swim around with lashing tails called flagella. The flagellates live inside a termite's intestines.

Like the bacteria that live in a cow's stomach and a rabbit's caecum, the protozoa break down cellulose into simpler chemicals called sugars, which the termite's body can use for nourishment.

Termites have a special problem that cows do not have. Once a cow has swallowed a few of the cellulose-digesting bacteria, they begin to grow and multiply in its stomach. Soon the cow has a thriving colony of bacteria, which it will keep all its life. But termites, like

A Germfree Life

Is it possible to live a germfree life? Scientists have conducted various experiments on goats, chicks, mice, and rabbits to find the answer.

When researchers experimented with rabbits, for instance, they found that being germfree made their caecum swell up. The caecum became so enlarged that the rabbit was unable to live and develop normally. Scientists realized that this happened because the rabbits depend on the bacteria that normally live in their intestines to supply them with vitamins. The bacteria also help to digest the cellulose in the grasses and other foods the rabbits eat.

all insects, have skins that are like armor and do not give them any room to grow. So they have to shed their tough skins several times during their lives. When a termite sheds its skin, it also loses the whole inside lining of its digestive system, from its mouth down through its intestines. And along with its old skin, it loses its whole colony of protozoa. Without the protozoa, it would starve to death. But the termite solves that problem. As soon as it has wriggled out of its outgrown skin, the termite eats that skin right up, including the protozoa.

The only way researchers were able to raise healthy germfree rabbits was to operate on them and tie off part of the caecum so it would not become so enlarged. The germfree rabbits were also given special vitamin supplements in their diet. They were fed foods low in cellulose and much higher in starches and sugars than rabbits eat in the germ-filled world. Finally, these rabbits were able to live healthy, germfree lives in sterilized chambers. They could even mate and raise their own young.

Plants That Need Fixing

Animals are not the only ones that have smaller symbiotic partners living within them. Plants that belong to the legume family, which includes peas and beans, have bacteria living inside them as well.

Like all green plants, pea and bean plants make their own food. But they need certain nutrients. These include carbon dioxide, a gas they get from the air; water and minerals, taken from the soil; and nitrogen. Plants cannot use the nitrogen gas that is found in the air. Free-living bacteria in the soil convert nitrogen gas to compounds that plants can

Nitrogen-fixing bacteria are an important part of the nitrogen cycle.

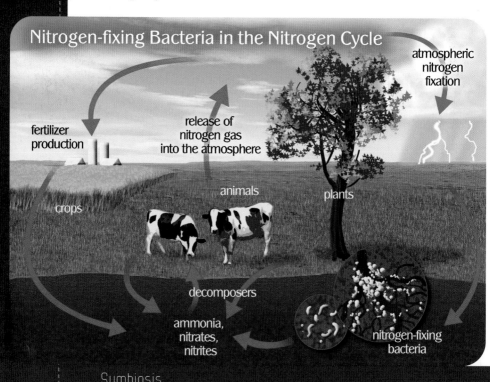

Nitrogen-fixing Bacteria in the Nitrogen Cycle

atmospheric nitrogen fixation

fertilizer production

release of nitrogen gas into the atmosphere

animals

plants

crops

decomposers

ammonia, nitrates, nitrites

nitrogen-fixing bacteria

use. These life forms are called nitrogen-fixing bacteria. Some soils do not have enough of these bacteria to supply the needs of plants. So the plants are unable to grow well in these soils. For this reason, farmers often need to add a nitrogen fertilizer to the soil to help the plants flourish.

Legume plants do not need to depend on nitrogen compounds produced by free-living soil bacteria. The legume plants take some of these soil bacteria into their roots. (Not just any old soil bacteria will do. Each type of plant works with a particular species of nitrogen-fixing bacteria.) Once inside, the bacteria multiply and spread like an infection. But this is a good kind of infection. The plant produces little growths, called nodules, that are filled with nitrogen-fixing bacteria. Nodule bacteria make more nitrogen compounds than the plant needs.

The nodules on the roots of this alfalfa plant are filled with nitrogen-fixing bacteria. Excess nitrogen from the plant seeps into the soil for other plants to use.

This excess may pass into the soil, where it can be used by plants that do not have their own nitrogen-fixing symbionts. Farmers will often plant pea and bean plants to enrich the soil so they can have productive crops of other plants.

Whales Can Help Clean the Environment

Could bacteria living in the stomachs of whales help to clean up oil spills and industrial pollution? Morrie Craig of Oregon State University thinks so. Craig studied the contents of a bowhead whale's stomach. He found that some of the bacteria in the whale's stomach could digest naphthalene and anthracene, two cancer-causing chemicals in oil that are difficult to break down. Other bacteria in the whale's stomach could digest PCBs, industrial pollutants that have also been linked to cancer. This would explain why bowhead whales can survive even when they eat food contaminated with PCBs and other poisons. If the whale bacteria can reduce the chemicals to nontoxic products, then whales can help clean the environment by breaking down oil spills that have contaminated the waters.

Good Fungi

In addition to nitrogen fixers and other bacteria, soil contains a teeming microworld of tiny creatures. Much of the soil life is fungi, which form a jungle of interlacing threadlike growths. These plantlike organisms do not make their own food. Instead, they feed on dead or decaying matter or live as parasites on plants or animals. Farmers and scientists have long known about fungi that cause diseases. Later, they discovered that some fungi form working partnerships with plants. These are the mycorrhizae that live around plant roots. (*Myco* comes from a Greek word for fungus, and *rhiza* is Greek for root.)

When seedlings of forest trees, for example, are planted in grassy soils, many of them fail to grow. But if a little bit of

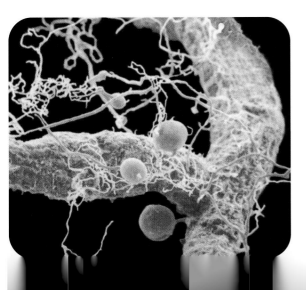

This soybean root has a mycorrhizal partnership with a fungus. The fungus takes nutrients from the roots. The roots use the additional surface area provided by the fungus to absorb more nutrients from the soil.

forest soil is added around the roots of the seedlings, they grow normally. Some nutrients the trees need are supplied by mycorrhizae in the forest soil. Scientists believe that the plant roots give out substances that the fungi need, such as sugars and amino acids. In return, the mycorrhizae change soil minerals (especially phosphorus) into forms the root can use and help to bring them into the root. Fungi may also help the roots to take in water.

Orchids have an even closer partnership with fungi. The orchid plants grow on trees in the forest,

These yellow and red orchids are growing on a tree with the help of a fungus.

using the tree trunks for support. Botanists have discovered that orchids will not grow unless they are infected with a particular kind of fungus. The fungi actually live inside the plant cells, but they do not cause disease. Instead, they provide food for the plants. The fungi are able to break down cellulose and lignin, tough materials from the tree bark, into simpler chemicals that the orchid plants can use.

Fossils of early plants show that they had fungus partners too. Scientists believe such symbiotic relationships helped plants to get established on the mostly lifeless soils that existed when plants first began to grow on land.

Bacteria are so important in nature that many species cannot live without them. But we would like to live without some kinds of microorganisms—the germs that can cause diseases such as strep throat, the flu, pneumonia, and tuberculosis. All diseases caused by bacteria, viruses, and microscopic protozoa are examples of parasitism.

Nature has two types of parasites. An internal parasite lives within the body of its host. An external parasite lives outside the body of its host. Both kinds of parasites can be very harmful to the host. But a well-adjusted parasite does not damage its host too severely because the host must survive for the parasite to spread. When the host dies, so does the parasite, unless it can quickly find a new home.

Inside Jobs

Not all parasites that live within the host's body are microscopic. Parasitic worms—such as hookworms, pinworms, and tapeworms, which live inside the bodies of people and animals—are not microscopic.

In fact, a tapeworm may grow to as much as 60 feet (18 meters) long *(below)*! It can fit inside its host because it is very thin and flat. The tapeworm looks like a long tape measure. Its body is made up of almost a thousand segments. Each segment can form new tapeworms. All the tapeworm does is eat and reproduce. A single adult tapeworm can produce more than a million eggs a day.

A tapeworm is a parasite and is dependent on its host for food. It uses hooks (above) *to attach to its host. It has no mouth or intestines and absorbs food through its body wall.*

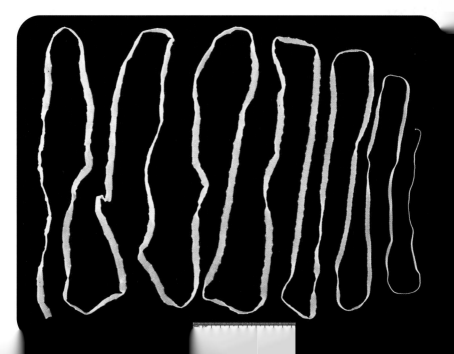

Cows and pigs may take in tapeworm eggs when they eat unclean food. The eggs hatch inside their intestines. The young tapeworms make their way through the bloodstream of the animals to their muscles. The infected animals can transfer these parasites to humans when the animals are killed and eaten as meat. These worms can eat so much that their human host often becomes thin and ill.

Medicines can be taken to kill tapeworm parasites, but it is best to avoid getting them at all by not eating under-cooked meat.

Other parasitic flatworms include the liver flukes of Asia and the blood flukes, found in tropical Asia, Africa, and South America. One type of blood fluke, the schistosome, infects about 200 million people. Like many parasites, schistosomes have a complicated life cycle. They live in the bladder and

Blood flukes like the one magnified below cause a disease known as schistosomiasis.

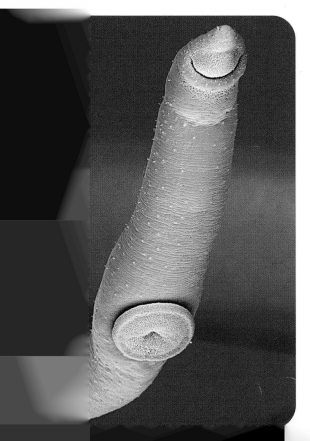

intestines of infected humans. Their eggs pass out with urine and feces and are carried into rivers and lakes. There they are eaten by snails and develop in the snails' bodies for a while. The young worms pass into the water and burrow into the skin of people who bathe or swim there.

Hanging On

External parasites that live outside the body of the host include ticks, fleas, mites, lice, and mosquitoes. These creatures survive by attaching themselves to the host's skin and sucking its blood. Their bites are normally harmless. But they may carry diseases that can be very harmful to the host. A dog infested with fleas can get seriously ill or even die. In either case, the fleas must jump off and find themselves a healthier host. Certain ticks can

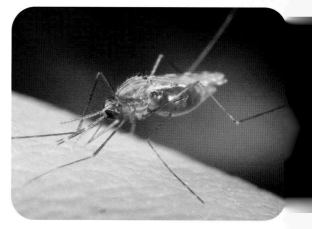

Mosquitoes often carry dangerous diseases. They spread them to humans when insects suck human blood for a meal.

spread diseases such as Lyme disease and Rocky Mountain spotted fever. Some mosquitoes carry single-celled parasites that cause malaria. If one of these diseased mosquitoes bites a human, it can transfer this very serious illness.

Double Trouble

The deer tick, *Ixodes scapularis,* feeds primarily on white-tailed deer and white-footed mice, but it will also latch onto a human if one happens to be handy. People who hike or picnic in the woods must take extra precautions to prevent deer ticks from attaching to their clothing or skin. Deer ticks are difficult to see and are only about the size of a pinhead. But when they suck an animal's (or person's) blood, their bodies swell up like little grapes.

A deer tick would not take enough blood to harm a person, but it may be carrying disease germs, especially the bacteria that cause Lyme disease. The bacteria do not bother the ticks, but when injected with the ticks' saliva into a person's or animal's blood, they can cause a flulike illness. If a person with Lyme disease is not treated promptly with antibiotics, more serious symptoms can develop. These include painful swelling of the joints (arthritis) and damage to the heart and nerves. Scientists have found that deer ticks can also carry germs that cause other diseases.

Parasites can also be found living among fish. The sea lamprey, a jawless fish that looks like an eel, flourishes in the Great Lakes. Its mouth acts as a suction cup and attaches itself to other fish, sucking the blood from their bodies.

Sea lampreys have killed many lake trout, whitefish, yellow pike, and blue pike. The Great Lakes fishing industry was desperate to find ways to get rid of these harmful pests. Scientists discovered that a special combination of chemicals kills only the larvae of young lampreys, without harming other fish. Using this chemical mixture and other control methods has decreased the number of lampreys in the Great Lakes by 90 percent. Some lampreys are still left in the Great Lakes, but the food fish are plentiful again.

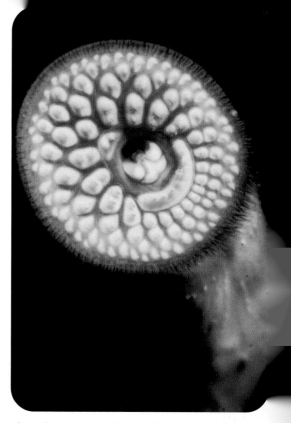

A sea lamprey uses its suction cup mouth (above) *to attach itself to another fish and suck its blood, eventually killing it.*

Human parents provide their children with all the basics: shelter, food, and protection. Plants and animals have the same needs that people do. But some animals cannot get what they need by themselves, so they form partnerships with other organisms to help them out. Animal partners may provide one another with food, protection, shelter, or a combination of the three. The partnerships may be very unusual, but because of the mutual benefit, neither partner minds the other's company.

Poisonous Protectors

Sea anemones look like unusual flowers with gently waving, petal-like tentacles anchored to the ocean floor. They come in a variety of colors—red, orange, green, blue, or a combination of these colors. But these sea creatures are actually very deadly to most fish, and their pretty tentacles are filled with stinging cells. When a fish swims near it, the sea anemone stings the fish with thousands of poisonous darts. It then carries its prey to its mouth, located at the center of the "flower."

Although sea anemones are very dangerous to most other sea animals, they form partnerships with some of them. One type of fish that is safe around sea anemones is the clown fish. This striking fish has a small, bright orange body wrapped with three white bands outlined with black. To avoid being spotted by predators, the clown fish hides among the sea anemone's tentacles. The sea anemone gets free food in return from its houseguest. The clown fish lures larger fish to the sea anemone. When the predator comes too close to the poisonous tentacles, it becomes prey to the sea anemone. The clown fish gets to feed on scraps from the sea anemone's meal.

Clown fish hide among a sea anemone's poisonous tentacles.

The clown fish is not automatically immune to the sea anemone's poisons, however. Scientists believe that it must build up an immunity. The fish swims close to the tentacles, without touching them at first. It then swims around the sea anemone for a while, touching the tentacles ever so slightly. Soon the fish becomes protected from the poisons.

If the clown fish stays away from the sea anemone for more than an hour, though, it loses its immunity and has to start the process all over again. And if the fish swims into the tentacles of a different sea anemone before building up an immunity to the poison, it will be stung and eaten.

Sea anemones are anchored to the ocean bottom and sometimes get sick when the water loses its oxygen and becomes stale. A clown fish may help its partner by moving its fins back and forth to freshen the water.

Hermit crabs also form partnerships with sea anemones. The hermit crab is a soft-bodied animal that crawls inside an empty shell that once belonged to a snail or some other sea animal. This borrowed shell becomes its new home until it outgrows it and transfers to a new one. Hermit crabs often camouflage their shells to hide from their enemies. The hermit crab may stroke a sea anemone's body until the sea anemone frees itself from the rock that it is attached to. The crab carefully lifts the sea anemone onto its shell and waits until its tentacles have a firm grip. The crab then carries the sea anemone around on its back.

This hermit crab has several sea anemones attached to its shell home. The anemones provide camouflage for the crab.

This arrangement is very beneficial for both animals. Not only does the flowerlike disguise help to hide the crab from predators, but the sea anemone will sting any enemies that come too close. Meanwhile, the sea anemone can catch more food by moving around with the crab than if it stayed in one place. When the crab tears and eats prey, the sea anemone shares the meal.

When the hermit crab outgrows its shell, its partnership with the sea anemone does not end. Once the crab crawls into a new shell, it transfers its companion to it.

Some other crabs put sea anemones on their claws for protection. The crab looks for two small sea anemones and puts one on each claw. It then holds its claws the way a prizefighter holds up his gloves for a fight. For this reason, such crabs are sometimes called boxing crabs. When an enemy approaches, the crab hits it with one of the sea anemones. In this way, it can protect itself or gain food for itself and its partner.

An animal related to the jellyfish, called the Portuguese man-of-war, is another attractive sea animal that has a poisonous weapon to capture prey and uses that weapon to help partners in need. The man-of-war floats on the surface of the water, held up by an air-filled bubble. Long, streaming tentacles dangle from its underside. Some of the tentacles are as much as 60 feet (18 m) long! Like those of the sea anemone, the tentacles of the man-of-war are armed with poisonous stingers and are deadly to any fish that touches them. But certain small fish, such as the brightly colored Nomeus and the horse mackerel, can live safely among the tentacles. The small fish lure bigger fish to their partner's deadly trap, and everyone can enjoy a good meal.

Hiding from Danger

A crab may also hide from enemies by putting a piece of red sponge on its back. The crab must hold it there until the sponge grows, eventually covering the crab's shell. Crabs that use this kind of camouflage are called sponge crabs. Since the crab looks like a sponge, fish ignore it because fish do not eat sponges.

Like the sea anemone, the sponge is able to get more food when it is moving around than when it remains in one place. Sponges eat tiny bits of food from the water that flows through the many channels in their bodies. When they stay in one area, they may use up all the food in the nearby water. The crab carries its sponge into new, food-filled water and also provides some tasty bits for the sponge when it tears and eats its own prey.

Seeing-Eye Fish
Everyone has heard about Seeing Eye dogs, but what about seeing-eye fish? A species of shrimp that is completely blind survives by living with a goby fish. If the shrimp wants to look for food, it taps on the goby fish and grabs onto its partner with its claw. The goby guides the shrimp on the hunt. In

This shrimp helps a goby by creating a hole for them both to hide in when danger comes. In return, the goby fish finds food for the shrimp.

return, the blind shrimp provides shelter for the goby fish by digging a cave in the sand, large enough for both the shrimp and the goby. The blind shrimp sometimes stays home while the goby goes out to get food to bring back.

The Hitchhiker

The remora fish is an underwater hitchhiker. It has a suction cup on top of its head and enjoys free rides when it uses the powerful sucker to attach itself to a shark that swims near. For this reason, the remora has earned the nickname suckerfish or shark sucker.

Their partnership is commensal because only the remora benefits, but the shark is not harmed. The remora does not suck the shark's blood as the sea lamprey does to fish. The remora sometimes

Two remoras get a free ride on the underside of this green turtle. They may also get scraps of food when the turtle feeds.

gets a free meal along with its free ride. When the shark
catches a fish, the remora detaches itself and feasts on the
leftovers. The shark also serves as the remora's protector, since
fish that might eat a remora are no match for the sharp-
toothed shark.

Remoras may also attach themselves to sea turtles,
dolphins, whales, or even to ships passing by. Although
remoras are accomplished hitchhikers, they are also very
capable swimmers on their own. But they prefer the easier life,
hanging around a big, strong protector.

Not all hitchhikers are good swimmers. Barnacles are
small, cup-shaped shelled animals that attach their suction
cups onto almost anything—turtles, snails, clams, fish, whales,

These barnacles have made their home on a humpback whale.

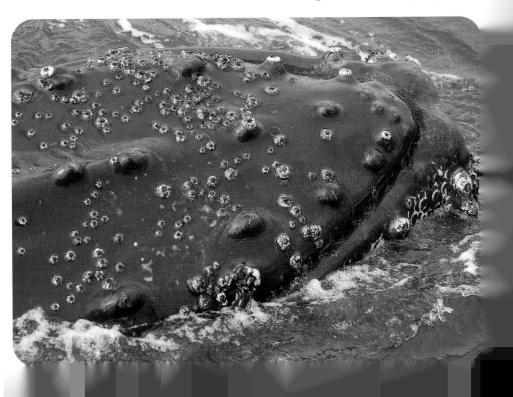

and even wood pilings or moving ships. Barnacles look like small lobsters when they are young and are able to swim around freely. But once they become adults, barnacles will settle down on a rock, a piling, or other object and never move again. They feed by waving their feet to send water carrying bits of food in through the opening in the shell. Barnacles that are attached to something that moves can find more food than the stay-at-homes.

Barnacles that settle down on ships often cause great problems for shippers. The tons of barnacles that build up on a single ship become so bulky and uneven that they keep the water from moving smoothly along the sides of the ship, and the ship slows down. Tremendous efforts and money are spent each year trying to scrape or burn barnacles off ships.

The Plant and the Ant

The acacia plant and the ant share an unusual partnership. The acacia plant is covered with thorns, which are often effective in keeping small animals from eating the plant. But the sharp, brittle thorns do not prevent large plant eaters from munching away. That is where the ant comes in. Ants protect the acacia against these predators. When an animal tries to feed on the acacia plant, the ants attack the animal's nose with vicious bites. Often the animal is annoyed and goes away.

An ant nest can be seen in the hollow thorns of this acacia plant.

The acacia plant provides its ants with shelter and food in return for their protection. The ants make their home inside the plant's hollow thorns. The acacia produces sweet nectar specially made for the ants, to bribe them to stick around. The nectar is very nutritious and satisfies all the ants' needs. The ants may spend their entire life on the plant.

When you were very young, your mother washed you often. Many kinds of animal mothers clean their young too. A lioness licks each of her cubs clean, and a house cat washes her kittens in the same way. A mother monkey picks fleas and bits of dirt from her baby's fur, and monkeys clean and groom one another even when they are grown. This helps to keep them healthy, and they seem to enjoy it.

A number of animals have cleaning problems that they cannot take care of by themselves. Even others of their kind may not be able to help them. Some of these animals form strange partnerships with other kinds of animals. These helpers actually eat bits of dirt and bothersome pests, such as insects, ticks, mites, and fungus growths, off the bodies of their larger partners.

Such cleaning symbiosis is beneficial for both partners. The cleaners gain a nourishing meal from the pests they remove. The animals that they clean also gain because the pests are annoying and can cause diseases that make the animals very ill.

Odd Couples

Cleaning partnerships can be quite surprising. The Nile crocodiles of Africa are among the world's largest and fiercest crocodiles. These huge man-eating beasts would not hesitate to attack anything in sight. But a small long-legged bird called the Egyptian plover is not afraid of the Nile crocodile. In fact, the crocodile welcomes the plover's company because of their special partnership.

Crocodiles live in warm, muddy waters that are filled with leeches and other pests. Leeches are small, wormlike parasites that use little suction cups to attach themselves to the gums of crocodiles and suck their blood. Crocodiles do not like these leeches, but they are unable to get rid of them. Plovers do like leeches— they like to eat them.

When the crocodile is ready to have its teeth cleaned, it sits on a riverbank, opens its enormous mouth, and waits for a plover to come by. The plover then hops in and picks through the

The Egyptian plover provides dental services for the Nile crocodile of Africa.

crocodile's teeth, gums, and tongue, looking for leeches or other parasites, and gobbles them down.

The partnership between the crocodile and the plover is beneficial for both animals. The crocodile gets a special cleaning service, and the plover gets a food source. The plover also enjoys the protection provided by one of the most ferocious animals in the world.

In addition to a cleaning, the plover also acts as an alarm system for the crocodile. With its keen eyes, the plover keeps a lookout for approaching enemies, such as humans. If one comes into view, the plover gives a loud warning cry and the crocodile dives for safety.

Other large animals—rhinos, hippos, elephants, zebras, giraffes, and buffalo, for example—also have

Rhinos often have birds for company. The birds clean the rhino's body of pests, getting a free meal in the process.

Cattle egrets wait on the ground for grazing cattle to stir up insects. Although they do not directly clean the body of the cattle, the birds do rid the cattle's grazing area of many pests.

birds that rid their bodies of nasty pests, such as ticks and other insects. Like the plovers, these birds may also watch out for enemies.

Most cleaning birds spend a lot of time riding the backs of their partners as they go to work. But an African bird known as the cattle egret offers a different type of cleaning. The cattle egret waits nearby until the animal kicks up the grass. Then it snatches up insects, especially grasshoppers, that go flying through the air. In this way, the egret actually cleans the area of annoying pests.

Underwater Cleaners

Animals that live in the sea have their own special cleaners. The wrasse is a small, brightly colored fish. It performs cleaning services for various kinds of larger fish, such as sharks, barracudas, moray eels, and other sea animals.

The wrasse has a pattern of dark stripes that makes it very easy for its clients to recognize. The wrasse gets the attention of its clients by standing on its head and doing a little dance to show that it is

A wrasse cleans the mouth of a sweetlips fish. Both animals benefit as the wrasse gets an easy meal, and the larger fish gets its mouth cleaned.

Copycat Cleaner

The blenny is a small fish that protects itself from predators by outsmarting them. The blenny is a copycat. It is not a true cleaning fish, but it looks similar to the wrasse and tries to copy its little dance. The blenny is so convincing that it is able to fool the client fish into believing it is an actual cleaning fish. The blenny can then get close enough to the big fish and eat its leftovers without being harmed.

open for business. When a larger fish is ready for a cleaning, it slows down and waits patiently for the cleaner fish to do its work. The wrasse swim inside its mouth and picks out parasites and bits of food from the larger fish's teeth and gills. Sometimes business is so good that there is even a waiting line, like cars in a car wash.

Farmers have important jobs in our society. They work very hard planting crops, helping them grow, and harvesting them so we can feed our families. In the insect world, certain insects have responsibilities similar to those of human farmers. Some beetles, termites, and ants grow gardens and gather harvests to feed themselves and their families. But unlike human farmers, these insects grow their farms underground. And their crops are not green. They are pale, whitish fungi.

Ant Gardens

In the tropical forests of North and South America, herds of ants can be seen walking up and down trees, carrying leaves over their heads like umbrellas. They are called leaf-cutter ants, or sometimes parasol ants. Each leaf-cutter ant has a large pair of sharp jaws, which it uses like scissors to cut off pieces of leaves or bits of flower petals. The ants carry these plant materials deep into the ground. There thousands of

Leaf-cutter ants carry back a leaf for their fungus garden.

worker ants of the leaf-cutter colony, each carrying away a grain of dirt at a time, have dug out caverns that extend 15 feet (4.6 m) below the surface and stretch out several yards (meters) wide. In each cavern, ants chew the leaves and flowers into a spongy mash. Then they lay it down on the floor to form a bed on which they grow their fungus garden.

The little ant farmers spread their fungi on top of the spongy leaf bed. Like any human farmer, leaf-cutter ants work very hard to keep their fungi growing healthy and strong. They dig and chew the spongy leaf mash and keep weed fungi from choking their crop, just as human farmers weed their gardens. As the fungi grow, they form balls, like miniature heads of cauliflower. They provide plenty of food to feed the ants and their families.

When a future queen ant leaves the nest to start a new colony somewhere else, she takes bits of the fungus along with her, neatly packed in a special pouch in her mouth. These will be the seeds for the new crop. This way, both the ants and their fungi spread to new territories.

Ants take good care of aphids so the ants can enjoy honeydew, a special mixture the aphids make.

Ant Cows

The leaf-cutter ants are not the only ant farmers. Other kinds of ants raise animals, similar to the way that human farmers raise livestock. They keep little ant cows, which are really insects called aphids. Aphids are tiny plant lice that can do tremendous damage to a human farmer's crops. Aphids suck the juices from plant leaves, stems, or roots. They may also inject poisonous saliva that makes the leaves curl or even drop off.

Bugging the Bugs

Aphids have another symbiotic relationship, even older than their partnership with ants. About 250 million years ago, bacteria called *Buchnera* found a home inside aphids. In return for food and shelter, the bacteria produced vitamins. Each aphid that is born receives a starter supply of the helpful bacteria from its mother. In this way, the *Buchnera* bacteria are passed from one aphid generation to the next. In fact, aphids and their bacteria have lived together for so long that they have become completely dependent on one another. *Buchnera* cannot live anywhere but inside aphids. And if an aphid is treated with antibiotics, which kill its bacteria, it too will soon die. The plant sap on which it feeds does not supply the vitamins it needs.

Another bacterium, called *Wolbachia*, also lives inside insects. But this partnership is one-sided. The bacterium lives as a parasite. Although the insect does not get any benefits from its houseguest, *Wolbachia* has effective ways of making sure it will be passed on. For example, in wasps, which can lay eggs without mating, the parasitic bacteria cause females to produce daughters, which will pass the bacteria on to their daughters in turn.

Farmers are desperate to get rid of these destructive pests. But ants would do anything to protect them. Aphids make a special sugar-water mixture that ants love, called honeydew.

Ants take special care of their aphid cows so they can have a constant supply of food. When an ant wants a drink, it strokes the aphid from behind with its antennae, like milking a cow, and drops of honeydew come out. Some ants build mud shelters for their herd in underground tunnels near the plant roots. Other ants take the aphids outside to graze on the leaves or stems. (Different kinds of aphids live on different plants. There are, for example, cotton aphids, oak aphids, and apple aphids. Somehow the ants know which plants the aphids prefer.) Some of the ant herders stand guard to defend the aphids against predators. The ants' vicious bites discourage most unwanted guests.

The partnership between the aphids and the ants is a good bargain for both. The aphids are fed, given shelter, and protected from enemies. The ants receive sweet, nourishing food in return.

Treated as Royalty

Certain species of the red ant have a similar milking partnership with the large blue butterfly. The large blue butterfly lays its eggs on the branches of thyme plants. The red ants see the butterfly's eggs and wait for them to hatch. When the butterfly larvae are

Red ants approach a blue butterfly larva to adopt it for its honeydew.
In return, the ants protect the caterpillar until it becomes a butterfly.

born, the ants guard the caterpillars to protect them from predators. For a while, the partnership is only one-sided. The caterpillars are protected, but the ants receive nothing in return. As the caterpillars grow larger, however, they begin to produce honeydew.

When a caterpillar is old enough, the ants do a little dance around it. They then stroke the caterpillar, forcing honeydew from its body. The ants love honeydew so much that they would do anything for it. So they treat their caterpillars as royalty. They provide their guests with a place to stay and plenty of food, which often includes the ants' own young! In return, the ants get a constant supply of honeydew.

The Sound of Music

We've all heard the sounds of crickets chirping outside, but how about caterpillars? Scientist Philip DeVries discovered that caterpillars of a tropical butterfly, *Thisbe irenea*, have tiny sound-producing organs. DeVries put a very small but powerful microphone in front of one of these caterpillars and recorded a chirping sound. The sound is too quiet for human ears to hear, but it makes an excellent ant caller.

These caterpillars feed on plant leaves and the sweet juices plants give off. When a caterpillar is threatened by wasps or other predators, it sends out chirping sounds that are similar to the sounds ants use to communicate. The ants quickly answer the call and act as the caterpillar's bodyguards, defending it against all predators. The ants stand guard until the caterpillar finishes its meal. In return, the caterpillar produces a sweet juice that is highly nutritious and rich in amino acids, which the ants can milk from its body.

The caterpillar eventually goes through metamorphosis and forms a chrysalis. The ants continue to guard and protect it, even though the chrysalis does not secrete honeydew. An adult butterfly finally emerges from the chrysalis, but its wings are wet and crumpled. As soon as the wings have dried, the butterfly flies away. If it hesitates too long, the ants will attack and kill it.

All green plants, including those on land and in water, have to make their own food to survive. This is done by photosynthesis. This process, as its name suggests, requires sunlight energy. Plants need water, carbon dioxide, and nitrogen compounds from the environment for photosynthesis. Using the energy of sunlight, these raw materials are turned into sugars, starches, and other carbohydrates.

Green plants get their color from chlorophyll, a green pigment that absorbs sunlight energy that can be used to power the chemical reactions of photosynthesis. The need for sunlight explains why many water plants live in shallow waters rather than the deep sea, which is without sunlight.

Shining Through

The giant clam, which can grow to more than 1 yard (0.9 m) long, has a symbiotic relationship with green algae, microscopic one-celled plants. The giant clam is so large and heavy that it can barely move around.

It typically lives in shallow waters with its shells gaping open, but it is quick to close them when enemies approach. The soft part of its body, called the mantle, faces upward toward the surface. Sunlight shines into the clam's mantle, and algae grow within small pockets in the clam's body.

Algae, like all green plants, make their own food by photosynthesis. The clam provides its algae with raw materials—water, carbon dioxide, and nitrogen compounds. In the sunlit mantle, algae can grow so abundantly that the clam can use some of them for food.

Photosynthesis is the process by which green plants make their food. First, sunlight interacts with the chlorophyll in the plant's leaves, and light energy is stored as chemical energy in small organs called chloroplasts. Water and carbon dioxide also enter the leaf. The carbon dioxide combines with water, using the energy stored in the chloroplasts, to produce glucose (sugar). The sugar is then transported to other parts of the plant.

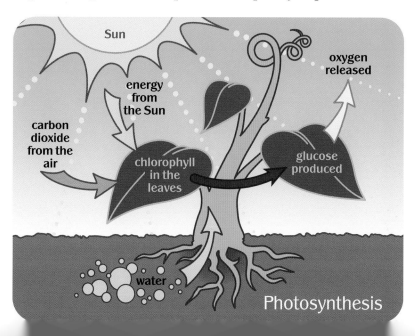

Sun

oxygen released

energy from the Sun

carbon dioxide from the air

chlorophyll in the leaves

glucose produced

water

Photosynthesis

All algae must have sunlight to live, but algae that grow in sponges have difficulty getting sunlight because sponges typically live on the ocean floor. Yet green algae thrive inside sponges that live more than 390 feet (120 m) below the surface of the ice in Antarctica. The sponges are able to capture the little light that reaches them. They pipe it to the algae in

A Case of Theft

Chlorophyll is packed in organelles (miniature organs) called chloroplasts inside plant cells. Some animallike, single-celled creatures that live in the ocean, called marine ciliates, steal the chloroplasts of the algae that they eat. After digesting the rest of the algae cells, they keep the chloroplasts intact and use them to make sugars in their own cells. Apparently this activity has been going on for a long time. In some cases, it has developed into a permanent relationship.

Researchers at Indiana University and the University of Pennsylvania have discovered that the single-celled parasites that cause diseases such as malaria and toxoplasmosis (an illness that people may catch by changing a pet cat's litter box) contain organelles that are very much like chloroplasts. These organelles much the same way as fiber-optic cables transmit light in high-tech communication lines and medical instruments. Sponges have a skeleton made of little glasslike spikes called spicules. Each spicule has a kind of cross-shaped antenna at its tip. Scientists have found that this antenna captures light, which then travels down the tube of the spicule to the algae living at the base of the sponge.

do not produce chlorophyll, but their DNA is very similar to that of plant chloroplasts. Each one is covered by a four-layered membrane, which is exactly what it would have if the parasite had eaten green algae and stolen their chloroplasts. The organelle has two layers of the chloroplast's outer covering, plus another layer from the alga's outer membrane. The fourth layer is the part of the parasite's covering that folded in over the alga.

The chloroplastlike organelles make special fats that the parasites need to infect their hosts. The researchers believe that the organelles could be a key to finding new treatments for these parasitic diseases.

Algae also play an important role in the formation of coral reefs. Corals are tiny, soft-bodied sea animals covered with stony skeletons made of calcium carbonate (limestone). The coral that is used to make beads and carved ornaments is actually the limy skeletons of dead animals. Living corals are known as polyps. When the polyps die, their skeletons remain. Most coral polyps live together in colonies. They attach themselves to one another and form coral reefs, which consist of both living and dead polyps. Coral polyps take calcium out of the seawater to form their limestone skeletons, which helps to solidify the reef. Coral reefs may come in different sizes, shapes, and colors, depending on the species.

Most coral reefs form in shallow waters where light can reach them. Single-celled algae can be found growing among the corals, where a symbiotic relationship develops. The algae receive the light and carbon dioxide they need for photosynthesis. They produce sugars and oxygen for the coral polyps in return. The polyps also use their stinging tentacles to capture and feed on tiny water animals, which provide them with important nutrients. The polyps share these nutrients with their algae, and the algae help them to form their limy skeleton.

The algae also provide color to the living corals, which may be yellowish, brownish, or olive green, depending on the types of algae living inside them. Sometimes, especially when the water is unusually warm, coral reefs may lose their algae and their color,

This coral has turned green because of the algae that live with it.

becoming whitish or bleached corals and, more important, sickly. Without its little symbionts, a bleached coral reef may take years to recover.

Corals have another kind of symbiotic relationship as well. Thousands of sea animals find shelter in the caves and crevices of the reefs. Colorful little fish, sea urchins, and various mollusks live quietly there, feeding on algae and hiding from predators. On the other hand, some predators, including crabs, moray eels, and sharks, use coral reefs as a hiding place to lie in wait for their prey.

Animal Shelter

Sometimes algae form partnerships with land animals. They have been found living in the fur of sloths, tree-dwelling mammals that live in tropical Central and South America. The

Partner or Prisoner?

The lichen was the first symbiotic relationship ever described. For years it was thought to be a perfect example of mutualism, with benefits for both partners. But researchers have found that the story is not quite so simple. When lichens are experimentally separated in the laboratory, the alga partner grows more quickly on its own and the fungus grows more slowly. These findings have led biologists to conclude that the fungus is really a parasite. But the relationship is good for both partners in harsh environments, such as bare, wind-swept rocks, where any algae that tried to make it on their own could not survive. In fact, the scientists could get the alga and fungus to join back together only when the conditions would not support either one separately.

algae make a home in the sloth's coat, using the sunlight for photosynthesis. The sloth does not benefit from the food the algae produce. But the algae turn the sloth's coat a shade of green, making the animal blend in with the forest, which helps keep it hidden from predators. When the leaves in the forest become dry and brownish, the algae also turn brown, keeping the camouflage effective all year long.

When three polar bears started to turn green at the San Diego Zoo, zookeepers became curious. Scientists discovered that algae were actually growing inside the bears' hollow, stiff hairs, making the animals appear green. Safe inside the bears' fur, the algae got plenty of sunlight and thrived. Unlike sloths, however, polar bears do not benefit when their white coats turn green since they usually live in the Arctic, where everything is white. This phenomenon has never been seen in wild polar bears, but cases of green bears have been reported in other zoos as well. Although the algae do not harm the bears, zookeepers and visitors prefer the polar bears to be white.

Algae growing inside this adult polar bear's fur have turned it green. The polar bear cub looking at it is still white.

The Birds and the Bees

People raise flowers for their beautiful colors and shapes and their sweet odors. Some insects and small animals are also attracted to flowers. They drink the sweet nectar the flowers produce. Flowering plants use visiting creatures to help the plants reproduce.

Some parts of a flower produce pollen, a powdery substance that contains the plant's male sex cells. Other flower parts produce eggs, the female sex cells. To form the seeds that will start off a new generation of plants, male and female sex cells must join. The joining process is called pollination.

In some flowers, pollen from the male structures (the stamens) simply sprinkles down onto a vase-shaped female structure (the pistil) in the center of the flower. When pollen grains land on top of the pistil, they sprout like tiny seeds. A hollow tube grows down the pistil until it reaches the egg chamber (the ovary). Then the male sex cells travel down the tube and join with the eggs, fertilizing them to start the formation of seeds.

Self-pollination, in which fertilization occurs within the same flower or in another flower of the same plant, has some disadvantages. All the seeds have the same heredity, and the new plants may not be able to survive if their living conditions change.

Cross-pollination, in which pollen from one flower is transferred to another flower, provides for more genetic variability. If conditions change, it is more likely that at least some plants in a more varied population will have the right traits to survive. The pollen of some plants is carried from one flower to another by the wind. But this is rather chancy. Most of the pollen grains land on the ground and are wasted. Cross-pollination is more effective when the pollen is actually carried from flower to flower by a bee, butterfly, bird, bat, or some other small animal. Over millions of generations, plants have formed many partnerships with animal pollinators. Gradually, the partners have become better adapted to one another. The colors of flowers are easily spotted by small creatures flying by, and their sweet scents also attract pollinators.

Pollination is the way plants reproduce. Many plants are dependent upon animals to carry pollen from one flower to another.

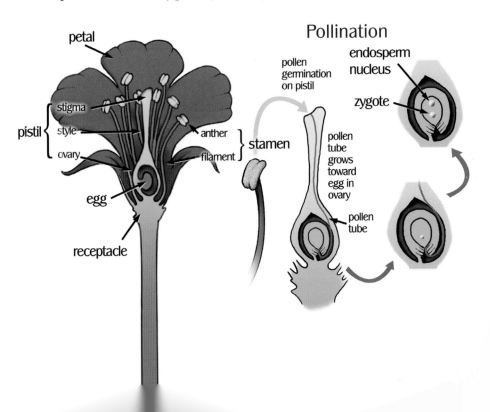

Often a flower's shape is perfectly suited to its most common pollinator. Long, tube-shaped flowers provide a good feeding station for long-beaked hummingbirds. Flowers pollinated by bees may have broad landing platforms, with the stamens positioned so that the bee brushes against them while it is collecting nectar. The bee collects some pollen in special baskets on its legs, but the powdery pollen also dusts the bee's hairy body. When the bee visits the next flower, some of the pollen grains fall off and pollinate it. In its travels, the bee continues to pick up new loads of pollen and spreads it from flower to flower.

Hummingbirds and flowers get along very well. The hummingbird gets nectar from the flowers and, in exchange, carries pollen to the flowers.

Symbiosis

Designated Pollinator

Plants are usually not very particular about who comes to pollinate their flowers. The yucca plant, however, can be pollinated only by one specific pollinator—the pronuba moth. In fact, these two species are so dependent on each other that neither could survive without the other. The pronuba moth does not collect pollen while feeding, as other pollinators do. Instead, it rolls yucca flower pollen into a little ball with its mouthparts and front legs. Then it flies off to another flower, drops the pollen ball onto the pistil, and packs it down. The pollen fertilizes the flowers, and seeds develop.

A pronuba moth is the only animal that can pollinate a yucca plant.

What does the pronuba moth get out of this partnership? A chance to give its babies a good start in life. Each time the moth pollinates a flower, it lays some eggs in the flower's ovary. The eggs hatch into caterpillars, which feed on the yucca seeds. Each caterpillar eats about twenty seeds, but the yucca plant is not harmed because the yucca flower produces about two hundred seeds. Some seeds fall onto the ground and grow into new plants.

Pollinating Fools

Most insects visit flowers for the flowers' tasty nectar. One kind of orchid, *Stanhopea grandiflora,* does not secrete nectar but manages to trick the euglossine bee into pollinating its flower. The orchid gives off a perfume smell to attract these bees. The bees visit the flower and collect the scent with their special forelegs, storing it in a pocket in their hind legs. While collecting the orchid's perfume, the bees transfer pollen from flower to flower. Some scientists believe that the bees use this perfume to attract members of the opposite sex.

Eating on the Run

Like most bees, hummingbirds also visit flowers to feast on the delicious nectar. But a hummingbird does not settle on a flower to eat. Instead, it hovers over the flower and eats while its wings continue to flap in the air. It pokes its head into the flower and uses its long beak to drink up the nectar. Meanwhile, the pollen sticks to the hummingbird's head, and the hummingbird carries the pollen along as it goes from flower to flower.

Tiny eight-legged mites, no bigger than a pinhead, take advantage of the hummingbirds that pollinate hamelia flowers in the rain forests of Costa Rica. The mites eat pollen and hitchhike to get from one flower to another. When a hummingbird sticks its beak into a flower, mites scamper into its nostrils and ride along when it flies to the next flower. The mites have a keen sense of smell. This allows them to recognize just the right kind of flower for another feast. The bird and plant get nothing out of this partnership. In fact, one mite can eat one-half of a flower's nectar and one-third of its pollen.

Humans have more symbiotic relationships with animals, plants, fungi, and microorganisms than any other species. We grow plants for food, clothing, and building materials. We raise animals for food, to carry burdens, or just to be companions to us. Although the lives of some of these animals and plants might be short, we provide them with food and shelter and keep their species going through the generations.

We also feed and shelter some animals, plants, fungi, and microbes unintentionally—in our buildings and even on and in our bodies. Some of them eat our food or goods. Mice and cockroaches, for example, hide in unnoticed cracks and holes and come out to pick up crumbs on the floor or raid the kitchen cabinets. The larvae of clothes moths can eat holes in a wool coat or sweater. Spiders actually help us by killing flies, beetles, and other insect pests. But some of our uninvited guests literally feed on us. In general, to survive, these creatures must be either very hard to see or able to get away fast.

Just Visiting

Some of the creatures that feed on humans live somewhere else and only stop by now and then for a meal. Ticks, for example, usually live outdoors and drop or crawl onto a passing animal for a meal of blood. When a tick is feeding, it buries the front part of its head in its host's skin. That sounds rather painful, but actually it is not. The tick's saliva contains painkilling chemicals. That is an important survival trait for the tick. To get a full meal, it must stay attached for hours, which could not happen if a painful bite attracted its host's notice.

Mosquitoes also feed on people's blood, but their attacks are of a more hit-and-run type. If you hear a high-pitched whining sound, then feel the sudden pain of a bite, you can be sure it was a female mosquito that got you. Only the female bites, to get nourishment for laying eggs. She can find you easily in the dark, homing in on your body heat and the carbon dioxide in your breath.

Some flies bite to get a blood meal for laying eggs. In many fly species, however, the adults do not feed. The immature flies— wormlike larvae called

Many fly species do not feed as adults, but they do when they are maggots (young flies, **below***).*

maggots—do all the eating. The mother fly tries to lay her eggs in something that is warm, moist, and rich in protein. That may be garbage, feces, a dead animal, or a cut or wound on a live person. One South American fly species uses mosquitoes as an egg delivery service. The female catches a mosquito and glues an egg to its underside. When the mosquito lands on a person's skin and bites, the egg immediately hatches. The tiny maggot crawls over to the fresh wound made by the mosquito and settles down to eat.

Unwelcome Tenants

The first bedbugs fed on bats that spent the daytime sleeping in caves. When humans began using caves as

This highly magnified bedbug, really only about .25 inch (.6 centimeter) long, enjoys a meal of blood.

dwellings, the bedbugs gained another food source. Their small size and flat bodies allow them to hide in cracks in the walls or in the seams of bedding and clothes. Young bedbugs feed on dirt and refuse, but the adults need blood, which they get by biting sleeping humans.

Fleas have also been sharing living quarters with people ever since humans first settled down in homes. The use of insecticides has just about wiped out the fleas that specialize in humans, at least in the developed countries. But the fleas from pet cats or dogs will also feed on any handy humans. Like bedbugs, fleas start out as larvae that feed on dust and dirt. The adults suck blood. Their fantastic leaping ability helps them to escape from a reaching hand. If you do catch one, its tough outer skeleton makes it very hard to kill.

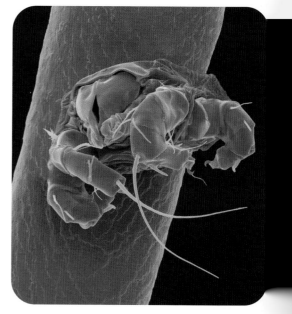

This magnified photo shows a dust mite next to a human hair.

Dust mites are commensals that feed on us, in a way, without ever actually being *on* us. House dust is a complicated mixture. It contains bits of soil blown in from outside, hairs shed by people and pets, fibers from clothes and bedding, and a surprisingly large proportion of dead skin cells. You may sometimes be aware of white flecks of shed skin from your scalp (dandruff), but actually, people shed skin cells from all over their bodies, constantly. This shed skin is called dander, and it provides a food supply for tiny eight-legged creatures called dust mites. Too small to see, they live in carpets, furniture, mattresses, and other cozy places. Usually dust mites live quietly without causing us any trouble. Some people, though, are allergic to them. When they breathe in dust containing mites or parts of dead mites, they may start sneezing or wheezing. People say they are allergic to dust, but actually they are allergic to dust mites.

The Dentist's Helper

If you have ever looked through a microscope at amoebas oozing along in a sample of pond water, you may find it a bit uncomfortable to realize that you have your own amoebas growing inside your mouth. No amount of brushing or flossing will get rid of them. The flexible tooth amoebas can slip into safety in the tiny spaces around the teeth. But these are not really unwelcome guests. They do not cause any diseases. In fact, they probably help to keep our mouths healthy by eating bits of food and bacteria that could cause tooth decay.

Life on the Human Landscape

If you were the size of a mite, you would have a very different view of the human body. Skin would stretch out in all directions like a great plain, with occasional hairs standing up like trees. The landscape would be dotted here and there with holes from which fluids ooze like water from a spring. Some of the holes contain high-calorie oils, and nutritious flakes of protein-rich skin are continually peeling off. It is not surprising that many tiny creatures have made their homes in this warm, hospitable habitat.

Unlike ticks and fleas—which may have a preferred species but will make do with blood from almost any animal that is available—lice are quite particular. You can't catch lice from a dog or a cat, and the lice that live on humans do not cross over to other species. Our prehuman ancestors were very hairy all over, and there was plenty of shelter for body lice. As people became less hairy, the lice had to specialize to survive. Some moved up to the head, others to the armpits or pubic hair. Some body lice survived by learning to live in the clothing people began to wear in cool climates. They continued to thrive until a century or two ago, when people began to bathe and wash their clothes regularly. (It takes a week for louse eggs to hatch, so Monday washdays got rid of all the lice hiding in clothing before the next generation could get started.)

Head lice are still a problem sometimes and can spread quickly through a group of young children in a school classroom or day-care center. The adult lice are small and colorless. They are not usually noticed until they lay their eggs (called nits), which are white and are firmly glued to a hair. Head lice eat skin cells, but they go down to the scalp only to feed. They spend most of their time up in the hair, clinging with clamplike claws so tightly that even washing will not dislodge them. The lice that live in the pubic region have adapted to warmer, moister weather than head lice. They are sometimes called crab lice because they look like tiny crabs.

Although dust mites do not actually live on people, a number of other kinds of mites do. Female itch mites burrow into the layers of dead skin on the surface and lay eggs there. Their feces can be irritating, producing an itchy rash called mange or scabies. Smaller mites, called face mites, live in the hair follicles on the face and in the oil glands that branch off from them. Unless a follicle becomes plugged and the multiplying mites get crowded, they do not usually cause any trouble. Surprisingly, face mites do not have an anus (the opening at the end of the digestive tract) and so do not produce feces that could irritate our skin.

In addition to the tiny animal life that roams over our bodies, our skin also grows a garden of tiny organisms—our skin microflora. Some of them are fungi, whose fibers lace through the dead surface cells of our skin and hair. Fungi grow best in warm, moist parts of the body, but they do not usually cause trouble. Fungi that grow too fast irritate the skin, which then sheds the dead cells faster—getting rid of the fungi. Occasionally the fungi grow faster than we can handle, producing a disease called ringworm. (Until the nineteenth century, people did not realize it was a fungus disease and thought it was caused by some sort of worm.)

Bacteria by the millions also swarm on the surface of our skin and mucous membranes. Some (such as *Corynebacteria*) are rod shaped. Others (including *Staphylococci* and *Micrococci*) look like tiny balls or strings of beads. Generally they do not cause any harm unless they get into the body, through a cut or scrape. By eating up much of the available food, these harmless bacteria help to prevent harmful bacteria from growing on us. The chemicals that our skin bacteria produce, especially the bacteria that feed on the substances in underarm sweat, help to give each of us our own distinctive body odor.

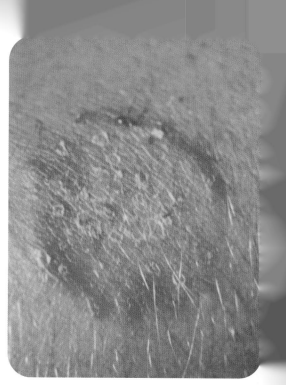

The rash caused by the ringworm fungus often looks like a raised red ring, as shown on this patient's arm.

A Free Ride

In the past centuries, people did not travel very much. Disease germs and other parasites tended to be concentrated in relatively small populations. Over the generations, the parasites and their hosts adapted to one another, so that once-deadly diseases often became minor nuisances. When people did travel, however, they took their parasites with them and exposed new communities to them. The results were sometimes disastrous.

Smallpox carried by sixteenth-century Spanish conquistadors, for example, wiped out the Aztecs, whose empire ruled Mexico. Measles was just a common childhood disease in Europe. It had a deadly effect on people in the New World when European explorers and settlers carried the germs to them.

Many scientists fear that we are facing another major threat from emerging diseases. So many people travel from one country or continent to another that a disease outbreak that started, say, in Hong Kong or Belize could rapidly spread all over the world.

When AIDS burst onto the international scene in the early 1980s, people at first thought it was a brand-new disease. But as old blood samples were tested and old records were scanned, the beginnings of the disease were pushed farther back—to the 1950s or even earlier. It seems likely that the disease passed from monkeys to humans sometime ago but remained isolated in small African villages. The breakout did not occur until changes in customs sent villagers into the cities, where they mingled with international travelers.

The combination of international travel and exposure to infected animals has brought other diseases to humans far and wide. When a highly contagious disease called Marburg hemorrhagic fever broke out in Europe in 1967, it was traced to African green monkeys from Uganda in central Africa. The monkeys were shipped to Germany and eastern Europe for research. Since the first outbreak, other Marburg outbreaks have occurred in the Democratic Republic of the Congo between 1998 and 2000 and in Angola in 2004. And severe acute respiratory syndrome (SARS) broke out in 2002 by exposure in Asia to Chinese horseshoe bats. SARS got a free ride through the air on international flights and eventually infected people in thirty-three countries. Doctors and researchers around the world cooperated to identify the disease and stop the outbreak from spreading.

The Marburg virus is highly contagious, so health-care workers must take precautions to protect themselves against the disease. This doctor is treating a Marburg patient in Angola.

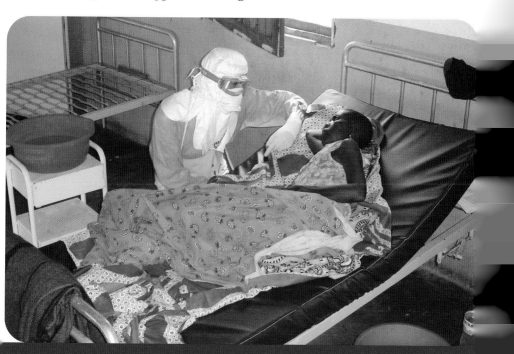

Space Wars?

When astronauts first brought back rocks from the moon, scientists worried that they might contain dangerous microorganisms. So at first, the rocks were placed in airtight chambers, with scientists outside the chambers handling them with gloves sealed into openings in the wall. Those precautions turned out to be unnecessary. No life was found on the moon rocks. But the dangers might be quite real if we someday send explorers to other planets. Scientists do not know what will happen if we ever meet truly alien life, but generations of science fiction writers have speculated about it.

Some think life-forms from other worlds would be so different that they would have no effect on us. Others say that we might be vulnerable to deadly plagues caused by alien symbionts. We might also be carriers of deadly plagues or at least contribute to changes in the ecology of other worlds we visit.

Efforts have been made to sterilize the space probes we have sent to other planets, so that they will not introduce microbes from Earth. But we do not know how effective these measures have been. If and when humans actually visit other worlds in person, there will be no way

This NASA scientist uses gloves and a sealed box to study a volcanic moon rock brought to Earth in 1971.

to avoid contamination. Every flake of dead skin we shed will carry life-forms from Earth, and so will every cough or sneeze.

In addition to the tiny creatures living on and in their bodies, space explorers probably will also carry other forms of Earth life with them. They may take seeds of food plants and

Scientists are careful to sterilize probes sent to other planets, such as the Mars Exploration Rover (above), *so that they do not spread disease.*

embryos of domesticated animals to raise in their new homes. They may also take along some commensals without really intending to. Ants, roaches, and other common pests will probably be hiding in some of the voyagers' supplies.

It is likely that mice will be stowaways on some departing spacecraft. These adaptable little creatures originally came from central Asia. After they began to take advantage of the food and shelter in human dwellings, they migrated to other places along with their human partners. Hiding in shipments of grain or other goods, riding in wagons and ships, hitchhiking mice spread to all the continents of the world and survived in the harshest habitats. During World War II (1939–1945), German soldiers in the hot African desert found mice thriving inside their tanks. Mice have also stowed away among the supplies of expeditions to the cold wastes of Antarctica. Meanwhile, new symbiotic relationships—both harmless and harmful—will continue to develop among the varied species of planet Earth.

Glossary

acacia: a plant that forms a mutualistic partnership with ants

aphids: plant lice; small insects that suck plant juices; may be cared for by ants in return for the sweet honeydew they produce

bacterium (*plural* bacteria): a single-celled organism without a nucleus. Some bacteria make their own food; others take in nutrients, some as parasites on a living host.

barnacles: shelled sea animals that attach themselves to moving or stationary objects or organisms

bedbugs: insects that suck the blood of sleeping animals or humans

bleached corals: coral polyps that have lost their symbiotic algae and the color they provide

blenny: a small fish that mimics a cleaner fish (wrasse) to obtain scraps of food dropped by larger fish

Buchnera: bacterial symbionts that produce vitamins for aphids

caecum: a pouch in the intestines; in rabbits it houses cellulose-digesting symbiotic bacteria

caterpillar: the immature form (larva) of a butterfly or moth

cattle egret: a bird that feeds on insects stirred up by its commensal partner

cellulose: a polymer made of many units of the sugar glucose; the main structure component of plant cell walls

chloroplasts: structures in plant cells that produce food by photosynthesis

cleaning symbiosis: partnership in which one species feeds on parasites that it cleans off the other species

commensalism: an association between organisms of different species in which one partner benefits and the other is neither helped nor harmed

cross-pollination: pollination in which pollen is transferred to a flower on a different plant

dander: flakes of dead skin shed by animals or humans

dust mites: commensal arthropods that are found in common house dust

Egyptian plover: a small bird that forms cleaning partnerships with the Nile crocodile

eukaryotes: organisms whose cells have a nucleus

external parasite: a harmful symbiont that lives on the outside of its host's body

face mites: microscopic arthropods that live in hair follicles and oil glands on the face

flagellates: protozoa that use whiplike structures (flagella) to move about

fungi: nongreen, plantlike organisms that feed on dead matter or parasitize living organisms

goby fish: a fish that forms partnerships with a blind shrimp species

green algae: single-celled plantlike organisms that produce food by photosynthesis and form symbiotic partnerships with fungi and various animals including sponges, the giant clam, corals, and sloths

herbivore: a plant-eating animal

honeyguide: an African bird that cooperates with animals to get food

hookworms: parasitic roundworms

host: an organism in or on which a parasite lives

hummingbirds: long-beaked birds that pollinate tubular flowers

internal parasite: a harmful symbiont that lives inside its host's body

intestinal microflora: bacteria and other microorganisms that live in the intestines of human hosts

itch mites: tiny arthropods that burrow into the skin, producing a rash called mange or scabies

leaf-cutter ants: tropical ants that cultivate underground fungus gardens

legume family: a family of plants, including peas and beans, whose roots form nodules that house symbiotic nitrogen-fixing bacteria

lice (*singular* louse): small insects that feed on skin cells in hair-covered parts of animals or humans. Head lice live on the scalp; crab lice are found in the pubic region

lichens: symbiotic associations between algae and fungi

Lyme disease: a disease caused by bacteria spread by the bites of ticks

maggots: wormlike immature forms (larvae) of flies

microflora: the microorganisms that live on the skin or in other parts of the body

microorganisms: forms of life too small to be seen without magnification

mites: small eight-legged arthropods, some of which have parasitic associations with animals

mitochondria: energy-generating structures in a living cell

mosquitoes: small blood-sucking insects

mutualism: an association between organisms of different species in which both partners benefit

mycorrhiza: a symbiotic association of a fungus and a plant

nitrogen-fixing bacteria: bacteria that convert the gaseous nitrogen in the atmosphere to forms of nitrogen that plants can use

nits: eggs laid by lice, usually glued to a hair

nodules: growths on the roots of legume plants that provide shelter for symbiotic nitrogen-fixing bacteria

parasite: the member that benefits in a symbiotic relationship that harms the other partner

parasitism: an association between organisms in which one partner benefits at the expense of the other, which is harmed

photosynthesis: the production of food (sugars) from carbon dioxide and water, using energy from sunlight

pinworms: parasitic roundworms

pistil: the female structure in a flower, including the ovary (egg chamber) that contains the ovules (female cells)

pollen: a powdery substance containing a flowering plant's male sex cells

pollination: the process by which plants' male and female sex cells are brought together to produce a new generation

pollinators: animals that transfer pollen from one flower to another

Portuguese man-of-war: a sea animal related to the jellyfish that forms partnerships with fish such as Nomeus and the horse mackerel

protozoa: animal-like single-celled eukaryotes

ratel: the honey badger; a member of the weasel family

remora fish: a fish that uses a sucker on its head to hitch rides on sharks

ringworm: a skin disease caused by the growth of fungi

rumen: the first chamber in a cow's four-part stomach, which provides shelter for symbiotic cellulose-digesting bacteria

sacred lotus: a flower that adjusts its temperature to help pollinating beetles

schistosomes: parasitic blood flukes (flatworms)

sea anemones: tentacled sea animals that form partnerships with clown fish, hermit crabs, and other animals

sea lamprey: a parasitic fish that sucks blood from other fish

self-pollination: pollination occurring within the same flower or flowers of the same plant

sponge crabs: crabs that form associations with sponges for camouflage

stamens: the pollen-producing male structures of a flower

symbiont: an organism that lives or cooperates with another species

symbiosis: a cooperative association between organisms of different species

tapeworms: parasitic flatworms

termites: social insects that feed on wood with the aid of symbiotic protozoa

ticks: eight-legged, flat-bodied arthropods that suck animals' blood

tooth amoebas: animal-like, single-celled microorganisms that live in the gums

Wolbachia: parasitic bacteria that live in insects and influence the sex of their offspring

wrasse: a small, brightly colored fish that cleans larger fish (clients) in tropical reef communities

yucca plant: a plant that forms a very specific pollinating association with the pronuba moth

Bibliography

Buchmann, Stephen L., and Gary Paul Nabhan. *The Forgotten Pollinators.* Washington, DC: Island Press, 1996.

Enger, Eldon D., and Frederick C. Ross. *Concepts in Biology.* 8th ed. Dubuque, IA: William C. Brown, 1997.

Facklam, Howard, and Margery Facklam. *Parasites.* New York: Twenty-First Century Books, 1997.

"The Greening of the Polar Bears." *Newsweek,* May 28, 1979, p. 60.

Knutson, Roger M. *Furtive Fauna: A Field Guide to the Creatures Who Live on You.* Berkeley, CA: Ten Speed Press, 1996.

Levine, Joseph S. and Kenneth R. Miller. *Biology: Discovering Life.* 2nd ed. Lexington, MA: D. C. Heath and Company, 1994.

Mestel, Rosie. "Codependent but Happy." *Discover,* January 1995, p. 89.

O'Toole, Christopher. *Alien Empire: An Exploration of the Lives of Insects.* New York: HarperCollins, 1995.

Perry, Nicolette. *Symbiosis: Close Encounters of the Natural Kind.* New York: Sterling, 1983.

Pope, Joyce. *Plant Partnerships.* New York: Facts on File, 1991.

Stein, Bruce A. "Sicklebill Hummingbirds, Ants, and Flowers." *BioScience,* January 1992, pp. 27–33.

Stevens, William K. "To Fight Away Wasps, Caterpillars Recruit a Phalanx of Ants." *New York Times,* August 6, 1991, pp. C1, C10.

For Further Information

Books

Beck, Alan, and Aaron Katcher. *Between Pets and People.* Ashland, OH: Perdue University Press, 1996.

Derr, Mark. *Dog's Best Friend: Annals of the Dog-Human Relationship.* Chicago: Chicago University Press, 2004.

Fleisher, Paul. *Parasites: Latching on to a Free Lunch.* Minneapolis: Twenty-First Century Books, 2006.

Goldsmith, Connie. *Invisible Invaders: Dangerous Infectious Diseases.* Minneapolis: Twenty-First Century Books, 2006.

Rhodes, Mary Jo, and David Hall. *Partners in the Sea.* Danbury, CT: Children's Press, 2005.

Sheppard, Charles. *Coral Reefs.* Saint Paul, MN: Voyageur Press, 2002.

Tackett, Denise Nielsen, and Larry Tackett. *Reef Life: Natural History & Behaviors of Marine Fishes & Invertebrates.* Charlotte, VT: Microcosm Books, 2002.

Zimmer, Carl. *Parasite Rex: Inside the Bizarre World of Nature's Most Dangerous Creatures.* New York: Touchstone, 2001.

Websites

BrainPop: Symbiosis
http://www.brainpop.com/science/livingsystems/symbiosis/
Information and a movie about the three kinds of symbiosis

Commonwealth Scientific and Industrial Research Organization (CSIRO): Introduction to Mycorrhizas
http://www.ffp.csiro.au/research/mycorrhiza/intro.html
Colorful introduction to mycorrhizas (associations between fungi and plant roots)—what they are and what they do

Flora of North America Association: Pollination Partnerships Fact Sheet
http://hua.huh.harvard.edu/FNA/Outreach/NFAfs_yucca.pdf
What kinds of pollinators and flowers work well together; the yucca
and the yucca moth; facts and more links

Gaia
http://www.kheper.net/topics/Gaia/index.htm
James Lovelock's hypothesis of planet Earth as a living superorganism;
Earth's organisms and their evolution

IDRC Books Free Online: Fish Culture in Ricefields: Rice-Fish Symbiosis
http://www.idrc.ca/es/ev-27767-201-1-DO_TOPIC.html
Discussion of the rice-fish food web and its applications in fish farm-
ing in Chinese ricefields

International Symbiosis Society
http://people.bu.edu/iss/
Information about the society and links to a photo gallery and a video
interview with Mary Rumpho, a researcher on a mollusk-alga
association

Lichenland: Fun with Lichens from Oregon State University
http://ocid.nacse.org/lichenland/
Introduction to lichens with cartoons, color photographs, and tips on
how to find, examine, and identify lichens

National Gardening Association: Creating a Pollinator Garden
http://www.kidsgardening.com/growingideas/projects/jan03/pg1.html
Facts and photos on selecting and growing plants to attract pollinators;
links to related articles and research tools

National Geographic Kids: Odd Couples
http://magma.nationalgeographic.com/ngexplorer/0601/articles/
mainarticle.html
Some examples of symbiosis; photos and links to a page on the clown
fish and "Best Buddies" e-cards to send to friends.

National Health Museum: Symbiosis and Co-evolution
http://www.accessexcellence.org/AE/AEC/AEF/1994/
bisaccio_symbiosis.html
Unit of activities for high-school students, sponsored by
Genentech Access Excellence

PBS Nature: Alien Empire
http://www.pbs.org/wnet/nature/fun/hive¬_flash.html
See how bees pollinate flowers

PBS Nature: Intimate Enemies
http://www.pbs.org/wnet/nature/enemies/partners.html
Feature on the tickbird and buffalo from a PBS episode on
lions and buffaloes

Smithsonian in Your Classroom: Plants and Animals—Partners
in Pollination
http://www.smithsonianeducation.org/images/educators/
lesson_plan/partners_in_pollination/pollen.pdf
Information and activities on pollination, including "Design
Your Own Flower"

The University of York Department of Biology: Research on
Symbiosis in Animals at York
http://www.york.ac.uk/depts/biol/units/symbiosis/intro.htm
Descriptions of some symbiosis research projects at the
University of York, England

Welcome to the Wonderful World of Insects
http://www.earthlife.net/insects/six.html
Click on "About Mites" to get more information on mites;
site offers lots of links

Index

Photo Acknowledgments

The images in this book are used with the permission of: © Nigel J. Dennis; Gallo Images/CORBIS, p. 5 (left); AP Photo/Ariel Schalit, p. 5 (right); © Stephen Frink/CORBIS, p. 9; © Gary Braasch, p. 10; © V. Ahmadjian/Visuals Unlimited, p. 11; © Mediscan/CORBIS, p. 13; © Ron Miller, pp. 14, 20, 65; © George D. Lepp/CORBIS, p. 17 (top); © Wim van Egmond/Visuals Unlimited, p. 17 (bottom); © Wally Eberhart/Visuals Unlimited, p. 21; © Science VU/Dr. M. F. Brown/Visuals Unlimited, p. 23; © Bohemian Nomad Picturemakers/CORBIS, p. 24; Centers for Disease Control and Prevention Public Health Image Library, pp. 27 (both), 29, 72, 77; © David Scharf/Science Faction/Getty Images, p. 28; © Science VU/Visuals Unlimited, p. 31; © age fotostock/SuperStock, p. 33; © David Wrobel/Visuals Unlimited, p. 35; © Mike Kelly/The Image Bank/Getty Images, p. 37; © Peter Pinnock/Photographer's Choice/Getty Images, p. 38; © Michael Poliza/Gallo Images/Getty Images, p. 39; © Alex Wild/Visuals Unlimited, p. 41; © Roger Tidman/CORBIS, p. 43; © Kennan Ward/CORBIS, p. 44; © Dan Guravich/CORBIS, p. 45; © Gary Bell/zefa/CORBIS, p. 46; © William Ervin/Photo Researchers, Inc., p. 49; © Ray Coleman/Visuals Unlimited, p. 50; © Jeremy Thomas/Natural Visions, p. 53; © Laura Westlund/Independent Picture Service, p. 57; © Robert De Goursey/Visuals Unlimited, p. 61; © DAVID LOH/Reuters/CORBIS, p. 63; © Ray Coleman/Photo Researchers, Inc., p. 66; © Michael & Patricia Fogden/CORBIS, p. 68; © Dr. James L. Castner/Visuals Unlimited, p. 71; © Dr. Dennis Kunkel/Visuals Unlimited, p. 73; Pierre Formenty/World Health Organization, p. 79; © Roger Ressmeyer/CORBIS, p. 81; © Getty Images, p. 82. Cover: © Gary Bell/zefa/CORBIS.

About the Authors

Dr. Alvin Silverstein is a former professor of biology and director of the Physician Assistant Program at the College of Staten Island of the City University of New York. Virginia B. Silverstein is a translator of Russian scientific literature.

The Silversteins' collaboration began with a biochemical research project at the University of Pennsylvania. Since then they have produced six children and more than two hundred published books that have received high acclaim for their clear, timely, and authoritative coverage of science and health topics.

Laura Silverstein Nunn, a graduate of Kean College, began helping with the research for her parents' books while she was in high school. Since joining the writing team, she has coauthored more than eighty books.